Testimonies for Jesus

for

By
Patricia A. Hart

Aspect Books

Copyright © 2011 Patricia A. Hart
ISBN-13: 978-1-57258-622-2
Library of Congress Control Number: 2011902245

Published by
Aspect Books

Preface

This book is written to encourage people who are looking for a stable church and loving atmosphere. It is written to encourage people to trust God. More than anything, this book is written to show how God has been with me every step of the way. These are testimonies to Him. He has taught me how to trust and how to pray and wait. I take no credit for any of the amazing things that are depicted in this book. I truly want the weary servant or friend to trust God and wait on Him no matter what the situation is. God is no respecter of person. Therefore, what He has done for others He will do for you and more, according to your faith in Him. Finally, Jesus' coming is very near, and He wants us to be ready.

Preface

Testimonies for Jesus

The Lord has done so much for my family and me. I would like to share some of the trials, pain, and weaknesses we have experienced, and the Lord's miraculous deliverance in my life. He has been my only help and comfort in every situation. May God help us to call on Him.

I guess I should start by telling you about my childhood. My dad was a very successful carpenter, but he did not manage his money very well and our family suffered a great deal because of it. I always believed he was a good person inside, but he was an alcoholic. Our weekends were filled with partying and drinking.

Unfortunately, the drinking led him to beat my mother much of the time. So, we were glad for the times he didn't drink. My mother had to get a job cleaning just to feed us. Our lights, gas, and water were off so much we expected it and accepted it. I was the fifth child of twelve. Many times we became the objects of our parents' frustration—beatings, angry words, and senseless searches for things that weren't even lost often took place. I used to think of it as Vietnam training!

We were abused in more ways than one. Somehow I began to think that it was the way life was supposed to be. As we grew up, we began to discover a new way of thinking. We needed a friend to help us and save us— that friend was Jesus.

One day my eldest brother and sister were discussing Jesus. As they whispered, I listened, wanting to know more about Him. They would not tell me anything and tried to hush me up. So, I went to my mother. She told me everything she knew. She was very gentle in sharing Jesus with me, and I knew she really knew Him. To tell you the truth, some of what she said didn't make sense, yet I listened. My mother spoke of Jesus in a way that would make you want to know Him. She also told me about hell.

Shortly after that time, my brother joined the church and we started to go. My eldest sister and I went a few times before we were introduced to the moaner's bench. The moaner's bench was the first pew in the front of the church. There we all bowed and they prayed for us. I really didn't know what was going on, but I decided that I would pray as well. I remember asking the Lord to come into my heart; I remember telling Him I loved Him. After much prayer, the deacons came forward and began to sing "Come to Jesus." Then they set out the old wooden chairs and said, "Come on to Jesus. Just come on up and sit in this chair."

So, we went up and took a seat. Now, I don't know about anyone else's heart but mine, but I really meant everything I said in that prayer. No one could have told me that Jesus did not love me and He had not accepted me. At the age of twelve, Jesus was my Lord and Savior.

One day after our baptism, my mother came to us and asked each of us what we felt. What did we feel? What in the world was she talking about? She drilled each of us from the eldest to the young-

I spent time deep in prayer and thought, seeking an answer from God...

est. I was really puzzled because I simply believed, and that was what I told her. She was not satisfied and accused each of us of not having a true conversion, and she threatened to tell the church. I was horrified.

In the days to come, I spent time deep in prayer and thought, seeking an answer from God as to how to respond to my mother and the assurance that I was saved from the point I asked for forgiveness. One night, as I bowed on our front steps, I prayed as I had never before. With tears, I pleaded with God as I sang these words, "The reason I pray so hard, I don't want to be lost..."

3

Suddenly, I experienced a fire that burned in my breast—a joy and a peace that I still cannot explain. I was filled with prayer and praise and tears of joy at once.

My brother was upset and tried to shut me up, but I would not and could not contain the joy I felt. Days later, I remember feeling a change taking place in me. Looking at my feet, I knew that I had new feet. Jesus was more real to me than I had expected. I later found Him to be more than sufficient for my life. I haven't been the same since that day. Guess what, the next time my mother told me I didn't have Jesus in my heart, I shared my experience with her, and she just smiled. Time moved on, and I continued to experience answered prayers.

My dad continued to come home drunk and fight with my mother. It was a miserable time for us. I remember praying for someone to take me away from our house. Sure enough, my aunt would come and get me. It seemed she needed a babysitter. Each time my request would go up, the answer would come. Over time, when I thought that I could not take the stress anymore, I'd pray and God would answer.

Life often brought problems that were too much for me, and I would turn to my mother for advice. She encouraged me to pray. My grandmother encouraged me as well. At one point, I was sent to live with my grandmother to babysit. My grandmother would ask me to read the

Bible to her. This made her so happy. She would tell me what I should pray for. She'd say, "Pray for a conquering faith."

My dad's mother told me about Jesus and shared all her magazines with me. The magazines had many testimonies of answered prayers. People would request prayer and the evangelist would pray. When God answered the prayer, the evangelist would record the stories in the magazine.

My grandmother, though a Seventh-day Adventist, never once told me anything about her faith. And my mother didn't make it any better, for when I questioned her, she simply said, "Oh, they go to church on the wrong day."

> *I loved the Bible verses and would repeat them often.*

I was given a New Testament Bible in the fifth grade. I really loved it and would read from it every day. I loved the Bible verses and would repeat them often. Mother loved watching Billy Graham, and soon I was taking Bible lessons from him. At the end of the lessons, their team asked me to make a commitment to do something for Jesus. They had listed things like singing, Bible reading, and prayer. So, like a child, I chose what I felt I could get out of—you guessed it, PRAYER.

One Christmas holiday, my sister was telling jokes. She had all of us laughing so hard. I was eating an apple while laughing and a piece of apple got wedged in my throat, and it really hurt. I went to my mother. She said to eat some bread, but that didn't work. My throat continued to hurt no matter what I did. I remember lying there talking to God, as He was the only one that could help me. So I took my Bible and placed it under my neck and asked God to remove the apple. As soon as I finished my prayer, God let a wind sweep through my throat and dislodge the piece of apple. I thanked God! Hallelujah!

Many other things happened after that time. I grew up, went to college, traveled, drifted into the world, and was raped. Yet, He was still there for me. When I was raped, I did not want to live. You can be sure I was not praying at that time; I was just drifting through life. I was realizing that life was not quite the way I thought. People were not kind, loving, and trusting.

One day I was crossing the street, not really caring if I got across or not. Suddenly a car sped off from the light, and came so close to hitting me, that it actually brushed my clothing. Then and only then did I want to live. I was determined to go though whatever I had to deliver my baby. I thank God for mercy and grace. I didn't deserve either, but I sure do thank Him, Amen! Truly, God kept me through it all. I am very thankful that God never left me. I must admit that even though I knew what prayer could do, I was not consistent in praying.

Later, I began praying for a husband—even though I was already a mother, God sent me a husband. After we got married, I found myself praying for strength and that God would help us grow and stay together. The Lord always made a way for us to manage with our eight children. God sent blessings through people and our business.

Yet, I was still praying for someone to help me understand what I was going through in my marriage. My husband was a great help to me at times, but he lacked compassion and sensitivity. I prayed nearly every night for this problem. I remember sitting on the front porch praying to God to send somebody. My husband had a bad habit of shutting down when we had issues to solve. He would pretend the problem only mattered to me, which would frustrate me more. I longed to understand why we were having that problem. And even though my children were pretty well behaved, I wanted to share my faith with them. My mother had shared enough about her faith through prayer meetings and church, and I wanted the same for my children. I just didn't know how to go about it.

One day a representative came to my house. He was selling Bibles and health books. I was impressed and ordered a Bible and a medical guide. Later, I returned to work and never saw the young man again. About a year later, while cleaning up, his business card fell out of some bills. I called the number and was connected with the storeowner. He promised to come over, and that was what he did. When he came, I was greatly impressed. He told me things I really needed to know. He offered words of comfort. As he talked to me, I realized that he was the answer to my prayers. In fact, he pointed me in the direction of more help and spiritual enrichment. Because of his patience, I began to understand the Lord's direction for our family.

After Benjamin delivered our first Bible story set, I recognized a change in my family.

Another reason for our stress was the fact that our church was having problems, such as financial and creditably problems with the leaders. We did not want to be involved, so we sought other churches to attend, even if it meant going out of town. We believed there had to be a church that actually practiced what it believed, so we began to search for a new church family.

After Benjamin delivered our first Bible story set, I recognized a change in my family. For one thing, my husband, never liked reading the Bible, yet insisted on me reading it. Then, he started reading the Bible stories and praying with us. We started having the prayer services I had prayed for, and we were happy. Soon, Benjamin invited us to attend his church, and we did. There was a meeting or revival going on. It was interesting. We hadn't overcome every problem, but God had clearly brought this man, Benjamin, to our home at this time. Benjamin and my husband hit it off really well, but Benjamin talked with me. He kept telling me that he believed I loved the Lord but I needed to complete it by keeping the Sabbath. Benjamin was the answer to my prayers, and he was not going to leave until he had made an impression on my mind about my love for Jesus in keeping His Sabbath (the fourth commandment).

Of course, I told him he didn't know what he was talking about because my mother had always went to church on Sunday and that was that. I had to check it out for myself. I cried out to God saying that He needed to tell me the truth because my mother kept Sunday but God said the seventh day was Sabbath. Boy, wasn't I ever crazy. I said, "If you don't tell me, I'm going to keep both days." When I prayed for the answer, it came to me in the evangelist's message. No one heard my prayer, only the Lord. Yet, the evangelist answered my request in an amazing way.

That same evening, the evangelist stood up and said, "Some people will try to keep both days!" He also mentioned the rest of my prayer. Only God could have told him what I had said. Eventually, I joined the church.

9

Later, something began to happen. Every day there seemed to be something new and brighter about the Sabbath message. I learned so much, and my sister accepted the Sabbath message. As I considered accepting the Sabbath for myself, there seemed to be a call to hurry up and accept the Sabbath truth.

Soon, I heard the call for people who loved the Lord and loved people to go out and carry the message through the printed page. There was a tugging at my heart to go up and join the other literature evangelists. Still, I hesitated. I thank the Lord God for calling me and for everything He has done for me. He put a joy and peace in my heart as I went door-to-door.

I am always saddened when the appeal is made to join the ranks of literature evangelists that the number joining are few. There is such a great need for more to join, and time is fast fleeing away.

I continued to work as a literature evangelist. My sister and I became very involved in spreading the message and helping others. But it was more than one or two people could handle.

Looking at my church experience, my eyes were opened to many things that displeased me among some of the members, and it broke my heart. I did not understand why I was becoming depressed nor why love and kindness was something detestable to some. Rejection from so-called friends, family and others was difficult to understand. Fortunately, the Lord God never left me—thank you, Jesus.

I have always been interested in the Bible—I love to study it and enjoy teaching it as well. Our churches decided to do an evangelistic meeting in the Jackson State area. I shall never forget those days. My sister and I were happy to help out. I always said that Linda representing *We passed out flyers and invited people all over the city to come.* love and I, Patricia, represented prayer. You know, Paul prayed and Silas song.

We were busy setting up the platform for the service and were glad to do it. We had discussed and wondered why there seemed to be a lack of closeness in the two church families. But we continued to do whatever we could to make things nice. We passed out flyers and invited people all over the city to come. Soon the day came. We had a dynamic speaker from California. He taught with such clarity that you wanted to bring everyone. And I really tried to do just that. I witnessed a miracle one night at the service. We needed to raise a certain amount of money, so the evangelist asked a certain amount of people to give twenty dollars to cover expenses. He prayed and we did to. Then they took up the offering. After it was counted, we discovered that we had the amount prayed for. So he asked each person that gave to stand. He was short one person and was puzzled. I told him the lady sitting next to me gave twenty dollars, but she had gone home.

My dad allowed me to use his car to take people to the meeting. So my sister drove my car, and I drove his. It was the last day of the revival service, and we were asked to fast and pray. I gladly answered the call to do it. It was no problem for me because I loved to do both. One day while sitting in the meeting praying and communing with God, I saw a light in front of us. It was getting brighter and brighter all the time. I tried not to look and held my head down as I gripped the folding chairs in front of me, continuing to pray. Suddenly, I felt someone peel my fingers up from the chair, and I found myself on my feet, hands raised in praise to God the Father. Praises poured from my lips, and I could not stop. Really, I had no desire to stop. I was caught up in a vacuum, encircled in light. Then a voice spoke to me, a soft, sweet voice ever so gentle. I cannot recall all that was said as I spoke to Him, but I know it was about the church and I remember saying that they must be crazy. At that point, I fell to my seat. Having no strength, I was empty and did not desire to say anything. The ushers asked if I was okay and if I wanted to leave. I did not respond. My sister sat there with me. She saw nothing and heard nothing.

Days later I was unsure of what to think of the incident, and I had no one to discuss it with as I struggled to make some sense of it. I had become very depressed and troubled because of the dreams I began to have. I shared one with my church family during the meeting. That proved to be the wrong thing to do, since the interpretation was mine (As I believed in my heart today).

I became aware of more dislike for me, and it became obvious that I was the subject of rejection. I did not understand why, and I became more depressed to the point of tears. One day a dear sister asked me why my heart was so heavy. During our conversation, she revealed the fact that a certain elder was talking about me. She did not know that I didn't know. It only made my heart sadder. Days went by, and I heard and was told things by people that I really respected. I had no idea they felt the way they did. One day while we visited a friend, he hurt my heart with what he said to me. My sister said she didn't care, but I did care. I heard the devil say, "They don't love you. I told you." I was crushed, and I wept uncontrollably. My husband was busy at our store. I had left my old job for the literature evangelist work. He did not understand what I was going through, nor did he have someone who could tell him. I was not eating, yet I continued praying, working, and witnessing door-to-door. However, I was drifting. I did not realize that my health was getting worst. I was not eating right and I was barely sleeping.

I began reading Ellen G. White's books, and finally stopped reading the Bible. I had no I idea that I was doing the wrong things. I stopped praying because I thought I had done something wrong. So much happened so quickly. The devil tried to take me out. We were invited to fellowship dinner, and that's when things seemed to really get confusing. The next thing I remembered was waking up at home, and my sister was with me. I didn't know what was happening. It seemed that I was very tired, depressed, and in a daze. My husband was visited by the pastor and elders—their visit was not discussed with me until many months later—but the discussion was not about my health.

Somehow I managed to drive my children back and forth to my sister's house that we always took to church. Her husband did not care for me because I was the one who took her to church. He was a drug user. One night while I was with her nothing made any sense. I was hallucinating and spiritual help was not available—the advice given to me made no sense and gave me no comfort. The next day my husband bought tickets for our family and others to be healed of whatever was wrong with us by a crusade evangelist.

We arrived there and were taken to the meeting. My husband did not know that we had been drugged. We found out later. The church welcomed us and made a big fuss of who would get the blessing for caring for us. They were so kind. I shall never forget them, and I know God will bless them for loving without dis- crimination. However, I witnessed many things

> *But I can say without a doubt that God was and is still in charge.*

happening that night. After the meeting, I had the strange desire to tell people things that were going to happen to them. The ministers prayed for us, and I experienced an electrical surge of energy as we held hands. In my reading later on, I discovered that this was not of God's Spirit. After we were fed and bedded down in this little house, I witnessed two young men coming down out of the loft. The wind was blowing so loud and my husband spoke to it to calm down. He strangely sat in the corner and gave me instructions.

There was so much that happened to us, and I will not tell you all. But I can say without a doubt that God was and is still in charge. Satan was trying to destroy us and no one was paying any attention to me, one of God's sheep. Many times we judge people and leave them alone to figure out why we are so unloving. How many times we refuse to receive God's children in His fold because

15

of their financial status, their educational background, or their family and spiritual backgrounds. May God have mercy on us as He works to save those who are unloved.

I started listening to what my sister said, and I doubted and blamed myself for whatever went wrong. I followed her and we took my children to Utica to stay for a little while. I could not rest—I kept seeing a sun going around the house, at least that was what I thought. Much earlier, I had visited my sister's house, and I believe I ate something with drugs in it—I remember eating cake but I can't remember what else. While I was in Utica, my aunt called my mother and told her that we were at her home.

Other strange things were happening that I was aware of. I observed a strange moon that seemed to follow me around at her home. I didn't talk too much at that time; instead, I thought about the strange things that were happening. I do remember being so exhausted. Finally, after much was said, we decided to leave for home. However, we were not able to get anyone to come to pick us up. I don't remember whose idea it was to walk home, but since we had gotten in touch with my husband and they agreed to pick us up along the road, we began to walk. As we started to leave, my aunt called to us, but we continued to walk, leading our children home. I had my Bible, and I began to read in Luke 9 (why that particular passage was so important to me I don't know). I turned to my sister and saw what appeared to be blackness. I thank God He kept His arms around us. At that point I was terrified, and we both ran across a field and I fell into a ditch with water in it. I remember calling on Jesus, and whenever I did, something seemed to pull me just a little closer to the water.

I don't know how long I was there, but someone suddenly pulled me up. It was my uncle. He called me and beat me in my side. I really don't think he knew or was aware that he was hurting me at that point, but he was. I did not say anything. I heard my sister speak, and then I opened my eyes and it was dark. My aunt in her despair had called the sheriff. She wanted us arrested, and the sheriff said, "For what? These young ladies haven't done anything."

We returned home with my husband, who had quite a bit to say. It was not good, but I didn't complain. He did not understand. My sister stayed with me; her husband could not be reached. She kept waking up insisting that we should leave and that God would lead His children. She said that often during the space of our ordeal. Sometimes I followed her lead, which took me into many now embarrassing situations. There are too many to mention. I don't blame her for whatever we had been given in our food, but it was clear that she had had more. That night my husband took us to the hospital. I was in one room and she, the next. I heard her crying out, and I tried to tell her it would be okay.

We wound up leaving the hospital and escaping from my husband. I did not question her when she said my husband had a devil. So we ran out of the hospital to get away. We hid under a bush and waited. My sister told me we were defiled, and I obeyed her when she said to take off our clothes. She said that we needed to run away, so I proceeded to do so. As I started to run, the small lamplight shone in my face, and I knew that something was terribly wrong. So, I picked up my bible and prayed to God with all my heart. I told my sister that God's people don't do those kinds of thing. She was not aware of what was happening. We redressed and I led her toward my home, which was not far away. I stopped at a fire station to use the phone to call home. My sister-in-law answered and sent my husband to get us. He scolded me and accused me falsely—he was so mean. He was probably more upset than anything. But I didn't say a thing. I knew he loved me; he just didn't understand.

Somehow, we ended up at my mom's house. My sister was still not well. She fell asleep in the den while Mom fixed food for us. I went to check on her, and my sister started telling me that she needed to go to the hospital because Mom and someone else were plotting to kill us and she had been poisoned. I believed her and called for an elder to pray for us. I started to tell him what was happening, but I broke down. All I could see was that my sister was dying and I had to get her to the hospital. So I called for an ambulance, and they came. My mother was furious. She tried to tell the paramedics that I was lying. They believed me and took both of us to the hospital. At the hospital they pumped her stomach, all the while complaining about of an awful order. At last we were sent home. We both were told to return to the doctor.

My husband took me to a motel to get some rest. Then we went back to the hospital where we spoke to a psychiatrist. He asked me, "What do you want?"

I said, "I just want to rest."

He offered me a room on the seventh floor. I did not consider that my decisions that day, having made so many, would affect my life until today.

> *I prayed that God would forgive them and that He would forgive me for anything I may have done.*

While in the hospital, I began to pray and witness. My first prayer was for whoever was responsible for my illness. I prayed that God would forgive them and that He would forgive me for anything I may have done. I began to read my Bible again a little at a time, and I prayed often. God sent my dad to visit me. He was so kind and spoke sweetly to me. I was impressed. I really appreciated that visit. God also sent my elder friend in the beginning to remind me to pray. Though he broke my heart with his words, I had no anger or bitterness toward him. (We all hurt and injure people with our words and have no concept of the damage we cause. Thankfully, God forgives us.)

In the weeks that followed, I was able to encourage others, and I actually saw a change in them. Many people in the hospital were having simple misunderstandings with their family members, and God used me to help them.

I spent one month in the hospital. I could see a lot of things clearer. God assured me that He loved me. He reminded me that it didn't matter if no one else loved me. He proved that to me every day by allowing me to see another day to be able to rejoice and give Him praises. And He continues to give me breath, which is truly more than I can ever thank Him for. His matchless love is amazing. Thank you, Jesus.

I was not prepared to deal with the effects of hatred when I was taken ill and finally hospitalized. But God was allowing me to see how the enemy works. He is real in the church, and Satan has done so much to destroy God's children. God allowed me to see what happens when we become so busy that we neglect prayer and our health/our bodies, which are the temple of God. He never left me alone. He sent people to encourage me, even in the hospital. He sent doctors and nurses who took time to check on me and showed me that real love does exist. God also reminded me that prayer and Bible reading were not something you could do to a point and then stop or read from a lesser light, which I had done earlier, not thinking that it was not wise. Neither did I think that I needed any rest. I simply was zealous to spread the truth of God's word.

I will forever praise Him. He raised me up and gave me back my mental strength and understanding. He restored my health. (I had lost a lot of weight due to continual fasting in a month time.) I thank God for keeping my family together and helping my husband to keep going. My sister left the church, and I prayer continually for her return. Fortunately, God continued to bless in our lives, and she returned to church. God also took care of our physical needs. He sent food and clothing to our home. He also brought a gentleman named Mr. Johnson into our lives. Mr. Johnson came by to inquire about my life. He told me he was a messenger. Then he presented me with an envelope of cash.

The enemy was angry because God was keeping us safe in His arms. We lost our business. The creditors couldn't wait, but we continued to pray. The more we prayed, the worse things got. On February 11, 1984, my car stopped running and our gas was turned off, but God always made a way for us to survive. We went through the Christmas holidays with no money to buy things for the children—spending our tithe and offering money was never an option. God again made a way. He touched the hearts of the church members, and they gave us gifts and fruit.

After my car was fixed it soon developed a flat tire. We managed to get the flat fixed only to find that it went down again. Sister Rudely and Ken helped us get home. That night as I prayed and mediated on the Lord's goodness to us, I picked up my Bible and began reading about Job's life. I must have fallen asleep reading, because I remember waking up to the sound of my father-in-law talking to my husband. The Lord moved my husband's family to give us food—they brought everything we needed and nothing that we could not eat.

In March 1994, our gas was turned off again, but we kept on going. It was obvious to me that Satan was trying to make us let go of God's hands. But he is a liar. We praised God and prayed.

Of course, being a literature evangelist was hard to do without a car, which we were in the process of fixing. Unfortunately, while my car was still not working, a bill collector came to pick up my husband's van. He took one look at my car and said, "We will just take this one."

I was disappointed because it made my work a little harder, but I chose to praise God that now I didn't have to pay for the repairs. The Lord God still blessed us. Unfortunately, all too soon, the troubles started again. Everything in the house began to break down. But we continued to pray and go on. I continued to walk to work and go door-to-door as a literature evangelist. To make ends meet, my husband sold what few beauty products he had at home.

> *I soon realized the devil was trying to make me feel bad.*

The year moved on, and a dear sister offered to pay my way to Huntsville, Alabama, for the annual camp meeting. She pleaded so much, and I finally gave in, although I didn't have any money or food. When we arrived, there was some misunderstanding about the rooms. It didn't seem to make a difference to them that I was the oldest or that I was a married woman and a mother. I was a guest for the first time, and I felt disrespected. I soon realized the devil was trying to make me feel bad. So, I encouraged myself with this thought, "You are a soldier, and a soldier can sleep on the floor. So what!" The camp meeting services were wonderful, especially for a down-trodden soldier.

After arriving back home, I learned that one of our

church sisters had something very special for us. It turned out she wanted to let us use one of her cars. I was very pleased, but then as I thought about it, I decided that I should spend time in prayer. While praying, I told the Lord, "Thank you, but we really need a car because I am a literature evangelist. I really need a way to get around town. I would be grateful for the chance to use someone else's car, but I really need my own."

One Sabbath morning, my daughter brought me her Sabbath School lesson. It was about Elijah and how he had prayed seven times for rain. Then, it came to me that I needed to do the same thing. So, I prayed again. Well, to my surprise, the following Sabbath the sister who had offered us the car approached us and said that she was going to give us the car. Praise God! He feeds us; He clothes us; He protects us; He walks with us; and He never leaves us because He LOVES US! Amen.

Hearing that the car would be ours, I could hardly wait. So I sat around the house and waited, but the car did not arrive. Then the Lord told me to go to work. I got up and went out to see people. (At this point in my ministry, I worked alone.) My last stop found me standing in front of a screened door. A gentleman spoke to me there, and after I introduced myself, he invited me in. When I took a seat, I noticed there was a second man sitting on a sofa behind the door, picking greens.

I firmly believe in God and trusted Him for protection. As I continued canvassing, I noticed that I was sitting beside his pistol. The canvass went well, and although he did not purchase anything, he later became my friend until he passed.

Around noon, I returned home for lunch and found the car parked in the yard, gassed up and ready to go. Praise God! Faith had sustained us once again. God was seeing me through. Amen!

We were so thankful to God for the transportation. Things began to get better: the church family helped us pay our gas bill. Then one day while canvassing, a case worker encouraged me to try for assistance through the food stamp program. My co-worker gave me a terrible time. My supervisor asked me one day how things were going. He encouraged us and proceeded to check into that situation. So, I prayed that morning that the Lord would take care of it, and I went on about the business for that day. Around three o'clock in the afternoon, my supervisor, Benjamin, picked up me and my husband and drove us right to the food assistance office. Praise God! In a few days the Lord God blessed us with more than a thousand dollars in food stamps. We had no idea we would get so much.

We not only received the food stamps blessing, but that morning I had visited my oral surgeon, and he had removed a piece of broken jawbone that was causing much pain to the point I couldn't work. When it was time to pay the bill, he replied, "No Charge." What a wonderful blessing!

I was so thankful; praise the Lord! As time went by, there was another occasion when we needed some funds. Shortly after praying for the Lord's blessing, we received assistance. God was continually answering our prayers. I can think of lots of times the Lord has blessed.

Then he said, "I can't pray for you nor can you pray for me."

They are too numerous to count. One day while canvassing, I saw a man sitting under a tree. He had his head down and looked sad. So, I said to myself, "I'll canvass him."

I showed him the Bible story set. He said that the books would not help him. When I couldn't persuade him, I offered to close with prayer. He then told me that he was a minister, so out of respect I asked him if he wanted to pray. But first he asked me what church I was from. I gladly told him. When he heard that I was a Seventh-day Adventist, he was furious. He told me that he could not pray for me. "Did you tarry?" he asked.

"What is to tarry but to wait," I said. I know some people are prejudice.

Then he said, "I can't pray for you nor can you pray

26

for me." In so many words, he told me that I was lost. I really wanted to slip away, but instead, I began to explain to him our beliefs. I did not come to give a Bible study; I did not even have my Bible.

I explained to him what the Bible says about the Sabbath. I started at the beginning of the Bible, telling him how God Himself had rested on that day and wants us to do the same. Then I told him how the Sabbath is also included in the Ten Commandments. The fourth commandment clearly states that we should remember to keep it holy. Also, Deuteronomy 5:12 says to keep the Sabbath day. He then told me, "Jesus changed that when He came because of those Jews."

I added that Jesus didn't come to destroy the law but to fulfill it. He also came to show the people how to love and live because the Jews had added their traditions to the law. God gave me the texts and clarity so that he could understand. I continued to Revelation 14:12: "Here is the patience of the saints: here are they that keep the commandments of God, and the faith of Jesus" (KJV).

The Bible contains the truth that no one can deny. Suddenly a light shown from heaven, and Elder Smith changed his mind. He dropped his head and said he was sorry. He told me that I worked for God and that I should pray for favor with the people.

There was a light shining around this man. Then he

27

prayed the most beautiful prayer. As I left, he told me that he had enjoyed talking to me. As I walked away, God reminded me of a song that very same moment; it was one the choir often sang: "Send your Holy Spirit right now." I was happy all day because I knew that the Lord had touched his heart and changed his mind. Of course, that is one of the many things the Lord has done in my life.

I recall another time when I was out in the field. I had made some serious decisions earlier about tithing. The same day, returning from the washer, I had prayed for some money. When I returned, I only had fifty cents left. As I folded my clothes that evening, Angela, my oldest daughter, came in to the house with a twenty-dollar bill. She said, "Look, mother! The lady next door sent this." She held out the twenty-dollar bill. This blessing came twice. The Lord God is good, and His mercy is everlasting. Amen!

Sometime after that, everything began to take a downward spiral. The bills began to pile in, but the Lord God always made a way for us to get them paid. One day as I was helping my husband at the store, a friend came in to talk with me. We were caught up in conversation—sometimes I am a bit careless—and I had taken my purse from under the counter and placed it on top of the counter. We continued to talk. In the midst of the conversation, I felt impressed that something had left me or was being taken. But I kept listening to my friend talking. I didn't stop to check it out. Soon my husband returned. As I was preparing to leave, I discovered that my purse was gone. You can imagine how I felt.

My friend was really upset. She kept telling me to look in her car—she really thought I suspected her. I didn't and I tried to assure her of that. My only concern was to get home. I needed to pray. She left and I started walking home. Along the path to our home, I greeted my friends and neighbors. They asked why the hurry, and I explained what had

> *I told Him that I knew He could give me back my purse because He had opened the Red Sea. . .*

happened and my need to tell Jesus. They waved me on. Finally, I arrived home. My children were having a good time playing. I called them together and told them what had happened. We kneeled down and prayed. After this, I had to talk to God myself, so I went into my bedroom. I turned to the east and knelt down and told the God of Abraham, Isaac, and Jacob what had happened. I told Him that I knew He could give me back my purse because He had opened the Red Sea and allowed the children of Israel to cross on dry ground. I knew God would help me. I asked Him to send the Holy Spirit to trouble the person's heart that had it, and I would praise Him for it. When I finished my prayer, I got up and went to a pay phone to try to close my credit cards.

Then, I went looking down the streets with Mrs. Tarzan and another friend. We even looked on her street. She later returned to her house. But I continued to search further down the street to the main intersection. As I was on my way back to the store, a lady came to her front door and said, "Come here." Once in her house, she preceded to tell me how her girlfriend had found my purse. She had found my purse on the outside of the store. I was relieved! She told me she knew it was mine because of the Bible leaflets inside. She reached into her closet and pulled it out. God had answered my prayers. I was so thankful! While thanking God, I offered her the few dollars that were inside my purse. She refused, so I offered to pray with her and that she accepted. At the end of my prayer, she fell on my shoulder, weeping.

All the money, papers, and credit cards were still in my purse. Praise God! Hallelujah! He is truly amazing. Since I had told my friends and neighbors about my purse while walking home the first time, assuring them that God would help me find it, I went back and showed the purse to them and shared my experience with them, including my church family. Books cannot contain the entire blessing that the Lord God sends us each and every day, but surely we can always praise Him for being there, alive in our mind.

Since my family somewhat depends on state assistance, we were given a caseworker. She seemed to be a nice person, but later it turned out she was untruthful. She really gave me a hard time when I needed assistance. So I decided to tell God about my problems, and He blessed me with a dream. I saw myself going to a hospital that turned out be a funeral home. At one o'clock in the morning, I awoke, wondering what it meant. Well, the next day I prepared to go to the hospital. But first I had to stop at my husband's place of business.

God blessed in ways we wouldn't have received if we were getting state assistance.

There I made some calls and discovered that I had been lied to by the caseworker. The individual on the phone gave me instructions of what information I needed to give to my caseworker. After going back home, I went to the funeral home to get copies of my medical records. So I went to the same places as in my dream. I continued to pray. Unfortunately, when I gave the documents to the caseworker, she became furious and proceeded to terminate me from all state services for food. Then again, God blessed in ways we wouldn't have expected, yet we got what we didn't ask for anyway. Amen!

Many things have happened since then, but one thing

is for sure, God has never left us. For example, our family was given glasses, dental care, and physical checkups at no cost. In addition, one of my children had a heart murmur, but I was unable to give him the medication he needed. Later on, we learned he had no serious heart murmur. Praise God!

The Lord continued to bless us, and on January 8 we were blessed with an 8 pound, 4 ounce baby boy. We named him Albert Hart III. He was healthy

"Lord, You know where that card is. If it's in the garbage, You know that too."

and another answer to prayer. I am truly thankful to God.

When we arrived home from the hospital, we discovered that the children had lost the mail. This was important because it contained a food stamp card worth $615. We looked everywhere. They had played all day and placed the mail in the chair in their bedroom while they continued to play. We even had them search the trash and under the house, but we were not able to find it. Then it started to rain. I remember being so frustrated with them, but I decided to go lay down because I was tired. Upon entering my room, I knelt to pray. My prayer went like this, "Lord, You know where that card is. If it's in the garbage, You know that too. You can get it back if it's Your will." Then I thanked him in Jesus' name.

It rained all week, but on the morning of the sixth

32

day, while throwing out leftovers, I looked out in the yard under the tree. There it was, the food stamp card on the ground under the tree, not even wet. Praise God!

Some of my neighbors were not so kind, but they were changing and I was too. One neighbor sent me a lovely vase of flowers she had made herself. I was so glad to get them, and as I was recuperating, it gave me plenty of time to pray. I began to sense an excitement that I could not explain. Then, in February 1987, my mother was blessed with twenty thousand dollars. I was happy for her, but I was hoping that she would send us at least a thousand dollars to help us with transportation. But it was not to be; she sent us only two hundred dollars. I had a hard time trying to understand this, but God kept speaking to my heart to seek out Jesus. I came to accept what she did. Besides, God had other ways to bless us as His children. I decided to wait on the Lord God for our transportation. If it's God's will, it will be.

I continued to witness, and I was glad. Thank you, God! A little later on, I went into business with one of my sisters in Christ. Unfortunately, we made some mistakes: it seems that the money was not there, but we still made purchases anyway. Shortly after we were in business and barely on our feet, we were concerned that we may not be permitted to receive food stamps because of our newly established business. I went home and prayed.

God answered our prayers: we were given permission to receive food coupons.

Unfortunately, my business partner brought in things we both agreed not to sell; things that were clearly against our faith. We could not come to an agreement, so I left the business. I was hurt, but I prayed that God would work it out between us.

I am not perfect, and I know I've been wrong many times, but I strive to do what is right. God continues to bless, not because I'm good but because He is good! He is wonderful.

During this experience with the business, he blessed me through the counsel of a very dear friend, Catherine. One time I was reading a Bible story dealing with forgiveness. At the end of the chapter, there was a test. It required you to write down all the people that had ever hurt you. I did. Then it said to check off everybody you had forgiven. I went down the list and checked them off, but when I came to my mother's name, I could not check it off. I even tried to force my hand to do it, but I couldn't. I wept. I believed that I had forgiven her, and yet I could not check her name off. So I called Catherine, and she told me to pray and fast, and she did it with me. Since I was not well, I fasted from TV, and I meditated and read the Word, and I did not talk on the phone for three hours. Praise the Lord; I was able to check my mother's name off the list. Thank you, Jesus!

I pray I can help her in some way because she has always opened her heart and refrigerator and pantry to my family. I don't deserve God's goodness, yet He is so very good to me. I love Him.

As I experienced the peace of forgiving my mother, I realized I had not completely let go of the situation with the business. It was still very painful, but after two months and a very interesting sermon, I let the Lord take care of it, and He did!

The Lord has been so good to me. Another time, He led me to two people, which I'll call Sally and Jim. They helped me grow in my understanding of people. There have been others who have helped me along the way, but these two people are special to me. Whenever there was a problem, we would pray and fast. God always gave us favor.

At one time, we were blessed to stay in our rental home, even when the rent was $810. Our landlord/lawyer gave us a chance to pay it off. Well, need I say more, God blessed us by helping us get the money. My husband purchased a car, and to be truthful, I did not want it because it was a 1975 Buick Electra. Nevertheless, I was thankful. I am reminded that no one can be everything; we only need God! The Lord God blessed our children with plenty to eat and enough toys to share.

The year-end convention was coming up, and I wanted to go. This was my petition to God. I remember asking Sister Mandy if she wanted to go, and she said she didn't have enough money. I replied, "I didn't ask if you had the money; I asked if you wanted to go." I asked her to pray with my sister and me. As we prayed and fasted, God answered. There was one other person who went with us who did not keep her promise—she made our trip somewhat unpleasant. But because Jesus lives, we made the best of our situation and were able to travel in a 1987 Cougar. We attributed the funds for the room, which came in after fasting, as a two-thousand-dollar blessing, for which my husband gave me two hundred dollars. The car and travel expenses came from my customers, who are my friends as well. They paid for their services and others were the result of the Spirit of God making impressions on the hearts of my mother and family as well. Remember, you have not because you ask not. Another prayer was to arrive at a certain time and be seated with my legs crossed when a certain individual would arrive. That happened as well.

Remember, you have not because you ask not.

I take no credit for these miracles, but I do declare that they are by God's goodness and mercy that they happened and continue to happen in my life and the lives of others. Praise God from whom all blessings flow. Amen!

Ready for the new year, my sister returned for work. She found out that there were many delays to slow her down. I have learned that the enemy will often try to discourage you or set up roadblocks. I have concluded that from all that has happened in my life even our best efforts can be overturned by deceit, strife, and jealousy— even among those who profess to be Christians. After the new year, I was informed that my disability papers were denied. I had been praying, trying to keep a right attitude, even though stress at home was mounting.

God knows how much I can bear. My one determination is to meet my Savior in peace. I continue striving to teach and train our children in the Lord.

Once again, our car troubles began. The transmission went out on our car, and we were back to the same point of finding another one. Somehow, I couldn't handle the mental and physical stresses. God helped me as I tried to get help again. Someone had to listen as I feared my bones and nerves were going to be damaged from the stress. One cannot describe the pain, pressure, exhaustion, and concern I felt and could not control. After many days, my supervisor called a meeting. As much as I wanted to go, I couldn't because of my health and the timing.

The Lord remained by my side and helped me to face the fact that I was soon going to be a mother again. In

March 1988 the Lord blessed, and I was able to see a therapist. I was denied a chance to go to rehabilitation, but God blessed, and I decided to let the disability issue go and all the questions I had. The hassles were too much for me. It was like repeated confusion. I had to answer the same questions over and over and no one believed me. My therapist said that I shouldn't give up. So Wayne Dowdy and his secretary helped me re-file my paper-work. I'm mentioning them because they helped me in my struggle—may God bless them.

Again, we were blessed with a baby boy. He weighed 8 pounds and was born at home. Believe it or not, it was the easiest delivery out of my ten children. We had trouble naming him, so we decided to draw lots to see who would get to name him. Our daughter Anna, who was named after a prophetess, was chosen. I prayed that God would direct her hand to make the right selection. She did; Josiah would be his name. I know that I'm unworthy of His blessings, but I'm so glad that God loves me.

One night I began thinking about how hard I make it for others to get back in good relations with me. I prayed that the Lord would help me. I know He will, because He knows just what I need. I talked to Catherine about my struggles. She is so encouraging—may God bless her. I know He will. Thank you, Jesus, for her and others.

At this point, I received a letter from the lawyer and

the judge. I prayed that the Lord's will would be done in this matter. October 5 was to be the day. I had to meet in the federal building. I had changed my mind and decided to file the paperwork after suffering so much pain. Now it was in God's hands. Looking back as I read these testimonies, God was and is always there for me. He was teaching me how to trust and wait on Him. He was teaching me to ask, believe, and claim. Why couldn't I see it then when it is so clear to me now.

A conference in Tampa, Florida, was coming up again, and I wanted to go. This time I asked to borrow part of the money from a friend for my deposit. She said that she didn't have it. I told her not to worry, that God had it out there for us, and I was going to find it. Not long after this conversation, my friend called me back to say that God wants us to tell the truth. She confessed that she had the money, and that I could borrow it. Again, God had the money; it was out there, and I was going to find it. Then something happened; my sister backed out. I let my fear of going alone get the best of me; I now realize that I should never give up because of other people. Perhaps it is a lesson that all of us should learn—never give up because of other people. We need to learn this lesson over and over again.

Sad to say, my health was going through some real changes, but I continued to carry on my work as a literature evangelist.

To top it off, our house was leaking real bad, and the owner would not fix it. We had talked about looking for another house, but neither of us had really looked. I guess I really wanted my husband to do it. It wasn't going to be like that. So, when we did look, the ones we found were too expensive. Then we went to the bank and were told our credit was too bad even for a repossessed home. Nothing worked, but when the rain started to come up the hall—it was already raining in the kitchen—I decided to do something. The house was not far from the church, but maybe it was too close to my mother. I was willing to risk it.

> *The Lord blessed us with a three-bedroom home with a fenced yard.*

Here is how it went: I asked my neighbors and they were not too helpful. I told the Lord about my problems during my prayer time, and the next day I received the owners name and number. Praise God! She wanted $9,000 for the house, but we prayed. After borrowing instructions from one of the church members about how to write contracts and legal documents, I drew up a letter of my intentions and offered her $3,000. I always read my notes to my husband, so that night I read it to him. He thought it was a big laughing matter, and he asked me why I had chosen three thousand dollars. Here's what

I said, "One thousand each for the Father, the Son, and the Holy Spirit." My letter made note of each item to be repaired at a thousand dollars apiece.

Soon she returned our letter. I remember being hesitant to open the letter. As I walked to my husband's business, I couldn't bear the suspense of waiting. I took the letter from my husband and read it. Her reply, she accepted our offer of three thousand, as is. Praise the Lord! The Lord blessed us with a three-bedroom home with a fenced yard.

Today, I am feeling bad. There is a pain in my chest, but with God's grace, I can make it. God always blessed me with a Bible study. A young man named Arthur completed the studies, although he tarried to make a decision. If only he knew the consequences of his actions. During one of our sections, God blessed me with another Bible study. His name was Raymond. He showed great interest and attended church with us. Raymond later accepted Jesus.

The Lord helped us get settled in our new house. He touched many people's hearts to help us. My oldest sister even called long distance to help us. We were having a hard time getting the gas on and making a deposit. She was kind enough to call and get it charged to her credit card. We were thankful. It was during that terrible coldness that I miscarried. Still, God was good and faithful.

We were still trusting in Him to supply all our needs. He changed the mean attitudes of those working at the utility company. (There aren't enough pages to record all of God's blessings to our family.)

One week it seems like everything fell into a slump. I felt like everything was pressing in on me. I was trying to finish washing, and in the process, I placed too many clothes in the washer. I had taken them out but did not realize some still had washing powder on them. I was using my mother's washing machine because, at the time, she lived next door. As I hung them up on the fence, I became more discouraged. Thoughts of giving up pressed in, and I started back to the porch. "Give up. Throw your hands up. You know you are tired," Satan said.

I felt myself losing strength, but suddenly Jesus spoke to my heart, "Don't you dare!" A strength came to my arms and legs, and I was able to zoom up the stairs and into the kitchen. I poured the clothes into the sink. I was praying and saying the 23rd Psalm. Before I knew it, the task was complete. On top of that, another sister blessed us by paying my telephone bill.

The literature rally was approaching, and this was an opportunity for me to make a new commitment. I started to work with the literature, and God greatly blessed me.

I am writing this story to record how God has blessed our lives. God, in His marvelous greatness, had not given up on our grocery business. For seven years, prior to the date we lost our former business, B&H Supply, we had been blessed to survive on a small income. With gifts and help from others, we were able to make it. We gave God the praise!

We also praised Him that we were able to get ten kids to vacation bible school. The devil didn't like that, so he messed with my car. It started acting up the same day

> *I prayed that God would be my judge and that Jesus would be my lawyer, and He was.*

as VBS. Thus, I found myself without transportation. To make matters worse, my 15-year-old child had run away from home because he didn't want to come in before midnight. His dad punished him, so he tried to walk to a church member's house. Somewhere along the way, he decided to get into a car parked outside of his house. The lady of the house saw him and shouted, so he ran. He was later picked up and accused of stealing and wrecking the car. We were horrified when we heard this information. He told us in the detention center that he only sat in the car and ran. We later found out that he was telling the truth. It was a setup, and we didn't have to pay any charges. They were dropped. I still couldn't believe that the owner lied about the car.

During this situation, I prayed that God would be my

judge and that Jesus would be my lawyer, and He was. We thought our son had learned his lesson, but he was constantly getting into little fights with his brothers and sisters. He became very disrespectful as we tried to keep him home like the judge wanted. We tried to hold him, and he tried to get free. He lied to us. Not only did he lie to us, but also lied to our friends. He even fooled my dearest friends. God never left us, even though it hurt. I was advised to let him go. I wanted him to understand it was Satan working in his life. Finally, he wrote me a note, "I am leaving, and DON'T COME LOOKING FOR ME."

It was not until then that I was realized the gang was influencing him. It was a terrible time, and I'm not going to mention all that went on, but when parents believe, neighbors, spouses, and friends don't. I cried unto God. God kept me sane. I prayed and God sent us to where he was. God told us that our son was at the club. My husband went in and brought him out. God became my very close friend. When all had forsaken us, God and only God sent us to where our son was. Jesus was the only one that kept me sane. I didn't find comfort in my husband, even though he was right there beside me all the time. This was a very, very, very hard trial for us, but God was our strength. Thank you, God! Thank you, Father! Thank you, Jesus! I will never be able to thank you enough for your goodness, blessed mercy, and amazing grace, for which I am not worthy nor my family.

During the time when these problems first started with my son, we were given an honor for successful child rearing. It was at this meeting that I, along with my husband, gave the honor and glory to God, for it was Him alone who had kept our family together.

On December 1, 1990, I gave birth to another child, a baby girl weighing 10 pounds, 4 ounces. God blessed us with this little girl, and we named her Deborah Elizabeth. Nothing is impossible or too hard for God!

The God I serve gives us so many blessings. He will not put us to shame before our enemies. I am 54-years-old. If I keep him first, He will sustain me! I love you, Jesus. Keep me in your care.

No matter the trials, the best you can do is have faith and wait on the Lord. The Lord has blessed and continues to bless. Angela and Fredrick are in college, and so am I!

As I end this book, and yet it is not an end, I will leave you with this message: God is faithful every day to supply us with everything we need. For me, all the wonderful blessings and answers to prayer have caused me to appreciate grace. It is God's gift to men. My pastor helped me in his sermon on prayer. I really understand now that my rejoicing over an answer to prayer may have been too shallow. I need to maintain confidence in God. God is always faithful to answer our prayers, even before we speak. So, until the day Jesus appears with the entire heavenly host, I shall expect an answer to my prayers, no matter how long the wait, and no matter what His answer will be. Jesus knows what is best for each of us. As an old song says, "Master, teach me how to wait."